Managing Products and Services

PS6

TAKING DECISIONS

Published for
The National Examining Board for Supervisory Management

by
Pergamon Open Learning
a division of
Elsevier Science Ltd

U.K.	Elsevier Science Ltd, The Boulevard, Langford Lane, Kidlington, Oxford OX5 1GB, England
U.S.A.	Elsevier Science Inc, 660 White Plains Road, Tarrytown, New York 10591-5153, USA
JAPAN	Elsevier Science Japan, Tsunashima Building Annex, 3-20-12 Yushima, Bunkyo-ku, Tokyo 113, Japan

This unit supersedes the Super Series first edition unit 109 (first edition 1987)

Second edition 1991
Reprinted 1993
Reprinted 1994

A catalogue record for this book is available from the British Library

ISBN book and cassette kit: 0-08-041655-1

The views expressed in this work are those of the authors and do not necessarily reflect those of the National Examining Board for Supervisory Management or of the publisher.

Original text produced in conjunction with the Northern Regional Management Centre under an Open Tech Contract with the Manpower Services Commission.

Design and Production: Pergamon Open Learning

NEBSM Project Manager: Pam Sear
Author: Joe Johnson
First Edition Author: William Tait
Editor: Diana Thomas
Series Editor: Diana Thomas

Typeset by BPC Digital Techset Ltd, Exeter
Printed in Great Britain by BPC Wheatons Ltd, Exeter

CONTENTS

Guide

USER GUIDE

1   Welcome to the User Guide

Hello and welcome to the NEBSM Super Series second edition (Super Series 2) flexible training programme.

It is quite likely that you are a supervisor, a team leader, an assistant manager, a foreman, a section head, a first-line or a junior manager and have people working under you. The Super Series programme is ideal for all, whatever the job title, who are on or near that first rung of the management ladder. By choosing this programme we believe that you have made exactly the right decision when it comes to meeting your own needs and those of your organization.

The purpose of this guide is to help you gain the maximum benefit both from this particular workbook and audio cassette and also from a full supervisory management training programme.

You should read the whole of this User Guide thoroughly before you start any work on the unit and use the information and advice to help plan your studies.

If you are new to the idea of studying or training by yourself or have never before worked with a tutor or trainer on an individual basis, you should pay particular attention to the section below about Open Learning and tutorial support.

If you are a trainer or tutor evaluating this material for use with prospective students or clients, we think you will also find the information given here useful as it will help you to prepare and conduct individual pre-course counselling and group briefing sessions.

2   Your Open Learning Programme

What do we mean by 'Open Learning'?

Let's start by looking at what is meant by 'Open Learning' and how it could affect the way you approach your studies.

Open Learning is a term used to describe a method of training where you, the learner, make most of the decisions about *how*, *when* and *where* you do your learning. To make this possible you need to have available material, written or prepared in a special way (such as this book and audio cassette) and then have access to Open Learning centres that have been set up and prepared to offer guidance and support as and when required.

Undertaking your self-development training by Open Learning allows you to fit in with priorities at work and at home and to build the right level of confidence and independence needed for success, even though at first it may take you a little while to establish a proper routine.

The workbook and audio cassette

Though this guide is mainly aimed at you as a first time user, it is possible that you are already familiar with the earlier editions of the Super Series. If that is the case, you should know that there are quite a few differences in the workbook and audio cassette, some of which were very successfully trialled in the last 12 units of the first edition. Apart from the more noticeable features such as changes in page layouts and more extensive use of colour and graphics, you will find activities, questions and assignments that are more closely related to work and more thought-provoking.

The amount of material on the cassette is, on average, twice the length of older editions and is considerably more integrated with the workbook. In fact, there are so many extras now that are included as standard that the average study time per unit has been increased by almost a third. You will find a useful summary of all workbook and cassette features in the charts below and on page vii.

Whether you are a first time user or not, the first step towards being a successful Open Learner is to be familiar and comfortable with the learning material. It is well worth spending a little of your initial study time scanning the workbook to see how it is structured, what the various sections and features are called and what they are designed to do.

This will save you a lot of time and frustration when you start studying as you will then be able to concentrate on the actual subject matter itself without the need to refer back to what you are supposed to be doing with each part.

At the outset you are assumed to have no prior knowledge or experience of the subject and can expect to be taken logically, step by step from start to finish of the learning programme. To help you take on new ideas and information, and to help you remember and apply them, you will come across many different and challenging self check tasks, activities, quizzes and questions which you should approach seriously and enthusiastically. These features are designed not only to make your learning easier and more interesting but to help you to apply what you are studying to your own work situation in a practical and down-to-earth way.

To help to scan the workbook and cassette properly, and to understand what you find, here is a summary of the main features:

The workbook

If you want:	Refer to:
To see which other Super Series 2 units can also help you with this topic	The Study links
An overview of every part of the workbook and how the book and audio cassette link together	The Unit map
A list of the main knowledge and skill outcomes you will gain from the unit	The Unit objectives
To check on your understanding of the subject and your progress as you work thorough each section	The Activities and Self checks
To test how much you have understood and learned of the whole unit when your studies are complete	The Quick quiz and Action checks
An assessment by a third party for work done and time spent on this unit for purposes of recognition, award or certification	The Unit assessment The Work-based assignment
To put some of the things learned from the unit into practice in your own work situation	The Action plan (where present)

If you want:	Refer to:
To start your study of the unit	The Introduction: Side one
To check your knowledge of the complete unit	The Quick quiz: Side one
To check your ability to apply what you have learned to 'real life' by listening to some situations and deciding what you should do or say	The Action checks: Side two

Managing your learning programme

When you feel you know your way around the material, and in particular appreciate the progress checking and assessment features, the next stage is to put together your own personal study plan and decide how best to study.

These two things are just as important as checking out the material; they are also useful time savers and give you the satisfaction of feeling organized and knowing exactly where you are going and what you are trying to achieve.

You have already chosen your subject (this unit) so you should now decide when you need to finish the unit and how much time you must spend to make sure you reach your target.

To help you to answer these questions, you should know that each workbook and audio cassette will probably take about *eight* to *ten* hours to complete; the variation in time allows for different reading, writing and study speeds and the length and complexity of any one subject.

Don't be concerned if it takes you longer than these average times, especially on your first unit, and always keep in mind that the objective of your training is understanding and applying the learning, not competing in a race.

Experience has shown that each unit is best completed over a two-week period with about *three* to *four* study hours spent on it in each week, and about *one* to *two* hours at each sitting. These times are about right for tackling a new subject and still keeping work and other commitments sensibly in balance.

Using these time guides you should set, and try to keep to, specific times, days, and dates for your study. You should write down what you have decided and keep it visible as a reminder. If you are studying more than one unit, probably as part of a larger training programme, then the compilation of a full, dated plan or schedule becomes even more important and might have to tie in with dates and times set by others, such as a tutor.

The next step is to decide where to study. If you are doing this training in conjunction with your company or organization this might be decided for you as most have quiet areas, training rooms, learning centres, etc., which you will be encouraged to use. If you are working at home, set aside a quiet corner where books and papers can be left and kept together with a comfortable chair and a simple writing surface. You will also need a note pad and access to cassette playing equipment.

When you are finally ready to start studying, presuming that you are feeling confident and organized after your preparations, you should follow the instructions given in the Unit Map and the Unit Objectives pages. These tell you to play the first part of Side one of the audio cassette, a couple of times is a good idea, then follow the cues back to the workbook.

You should then work through each workbook section doing all that is asked of you until you reach the final assessments. Don't forget to keep your eye on the Unit Map as you progress and try to finish each session at a sensible point in the unit, ideally at the end of a complete section or part. You should always start your next session by looking back, for at least ten to fifteen minutes, at the work you did in the previous session.

You are encouraged to retain any reports, work-based assignments or other material produced in conjunction with your work through this unit in case you wish to present these later as evidence for a competency award or accreditation of prior learning.

Help, guidance and tutorial support

The workbook and audio cassette have been designed to be as self-contained as possible, acting as your guide and tutor throughout your studies. However, there are bound to be times when you might not quite understand what the author is saying, or perhaps you don't agree with a certain point. Whatever the reason, we all need help and support from time to time and Open Learners are no exception.

Help during Open Learning study can come in many forms, providing you are prepared to seek it out and use it:

- first of all you could help yourself. Perhaps you are giving up too easily. Go back over it and try again;

- or you could ask your family or friends. Even if they don't understand the subject, the act of discussing it sometimes clarifies things in your own mind;

- then there is your company trainer or superior. If you are training as part of a company scheme, and during work time, then help and support will probably have been arranged for you already. Help and advice under these circumstances are important, especially as they can help you interpret your studies through actual and relevant company examples;

- if you are pursuing this training on your own, you could enlist expert help from a local Open Learning centre or agency. Such organizations exist in considerable numbers throughout the UK, often linked to colleges and other training establishments. The National Examining Board for Supervisory Management (NEBSM or NEBS Management), has several hundred such centres and can provide not only help and support but full assessment and accreditation facilities if you want to pursue a qualification as part of your chosen programme.

The NEBSM Super Series second edition is a selection of workbook and audio cassette packages covering a wide range of supervisory and first line management topics.

Although the individual books and cassettes are completely self-contained and cover single subject areas, each belongs to one of the four modular groups shown. These groups can help you build up your personal development programme as you can easily see which subjects are related. The groups are also important if you undertake any NEBSM national award programme.

Managing Human Resources

HR1	Supervising at Work	HR10	Managing Time
HR2	Supervising with Authority	HR11	Hiring People
HR3	Team Leading	HR12	Interviewing
HR4	Delegation	HR13	Training Plans
HR5	Workteams	HR14	Training Sessions
HR6	Motivating People	HR15	Industrial Relations
HR7	Leading Change	HR16	Employment and the Law
HR8	Personnel in Action	HR17	Equality at Work
HR9	Performance Appraisal	HR18	Work-based Assessment

Managing Information

IN1	Communicating	IN7	Using Statistics
IN2	Speaking Skills	IN8	Presenting Figures
IN3	Orders and Instructions	IN9	Introduction to Information Technology
IN4	Meetings		
IN5	Writing Skills	IN10	Computers and Communication Systems
IN6	Project Preparation		

Managing Financial Resources

FR1	Accounting for Money	FR4	Pay Systems
FR2	Control via Budgets	FR5	Security
FR3	Controlling Costs		

Managing Products and Services

PS1	Controlling Work	PS8	Productivity
PS2	Health and Safety	PS9	Stock Control Systems
PS3	Accident Prevention	PS10	Stores Control
PS4	Ensuring Quality	PS11	Efficiency in the Office
PS5	Quality Techniques	PS12	Marketing
PS6	Taking Decisions	PS13	Caring for the Environment
PS7	Solving Problems	PS14	Caring for the Customer

While the contents have been thoroughly updated, many Super Series 2 titles remain the same as, or very similar to the first edition units. Where, through merger, rewrite or deletion title changes have also been made, this summary should help you. If you are in any doubt please contact Pergamon Open Learning direct.

First Edition	**Second Edition**
Merged titles	
105 Organization Systems and 106 Supervising in the System	HR1 Supervising at Work
100 Needs and Rewards and 101 Enriching Work	HR6 Motivating People
502 Discipline and the Law and 508 Supervising and the Law	HR16 Employment and the Law
204 Easy Statistics and 213 Descriptive Statistics	IN7 Using Statistics
200 Looking at Figures and 202 Using Graphs	IN8 Presenting Figures
210 Computers and 303 Communication Systems	IN10 Computers and Communication Systems
402 Cost Reduction and 405 Cost Centres	FR3 Controlling Costs
203 Method Study and 208 Value Analysis	PS8 Productivity
Major title changes	
209 Quality Circles	PS4 Ensuring Quality
205 Quality Control	PS5 Quality Techniques
Deleted titles	
406 National Economy/410 Single European Market	

The NEBSM Super Series 2 Open Learning material is published by Pergamon Open Learning in conjunction with NEBS Management.

NEBS Management is the largest provider of management education, training courses and qualifications in the United Kingdom, operating through over 700 Centres. Many of these Centres offer Open Learning and can provide help to individual students.

Many thousands of students follow the Open Learning route with great success and gain NEBSM or other qualifications.

NEBSM maintains a twin track approach to Supervisory Management training offering knowledge-based awards at three levels:

● the NEBSM Introductory Award in Supervisory Management;
● the NEBSM Certificate in Supervisory Management;
● the NEBSM Diploma in Supervisory Management;

and competence based awards at two levels:

● the NEBSM NVQ in Supervisory Management at Level 3;
● the NEBSM NVQ in Management at Level 4.

Knowledge-based awards and Super Series 2

The **_Introductory Award_** requires a minimum of 30 hours of study and provides a grounding in the theory and practice of supervisory management. An agreed programme of up to five NEBSM Super Series 2 units plus a one-day workshop satisfactorily completed can lead to this Award. Pre-approved topic combinations exist for general, industrial and commercial options. Completed Super Series 2 units can be allowed as an exemption towards the full NEBSM Certificate.

The **_Certificate in Supervisory Management_** requires study of up to 23 NEBSM Super Series 2 units and participation in group activity or workshops. The assessment system includes work-based assignments, a case study, a project and an oral interview. The certificate is divided into four modules and each one may be completed separately.
A **_Module Award_** can be made on successful completion of each module, and when the assessments are satisfactorily completed the Certificate is awarded. Students will need to register with a NEBSM Centre in order to enter for an award; NEBSM can advise you.

The **_Diploma in Supervisory Management_** consists of the formulation and implementation of a Personal Development Plan plus a generic management core. The programme is assessed by means of a log book, case study/in tray exercises, project or presentation.

The NEBSM Super Series 2 Open Learning material is designed for use at Certificate level but can also be used for the Introductory Award and provide valuable background knowledge for the Diploma.

| Competence-based programmes and Super Series 2 | The **NEBSM NVQ in Supervisory Management Level 3** is based upon the seven units of competence produced by the Management Charter Initiative (MCI) in their publication *Supervisory Management Standards* of June 1992. It is recognized by the National Council for Vocational Qualifications (NCVQ) at Level 3 in their framework. |

The **NEBSM NVQ in Management Level 4** is based upon the nine units of competence produced by MCI in their publication *Occupational Standards for Managers, Management 1 and Assessment Criteria* of April 1991. It is recognized by the National Council for Vocational Qualifications (NCVQ) at Level 4 in their framework.

Super Series 2 units can be used to provide the necessary underpinning knowledge, skills and understanding that are required to prepare yourself for competence-based assessment.

Working through Super Series 2 units cannot, by itself, provide you with everything you need to enter or be entered for competence assessment. This must come from a combination of skill, experience and knowledge gained both on and off the job.

You will also find many of the 47 Super Series 2 units of use in learning programmes for other National Vocational Qualifications (NVQs) which include elements of supervisory management. Please check with the relevant NVQ lead body for information on Units of Competence and underlying knowledge, skills and understanding.

Competence Match Chart

The Competence Match Chart overleaf illustrates which Super Series 2 titles provide background vital to the current MCI M1S Supervisory Management Standards. You will also find that there is similar matching at MCI M1, Management 1 Standards. This is shown on the chart on page xiii.

For more information about MCI contact:

Management Charter Initiative
Russell Square House
10–12 Russell Square
London
WC1B 5BZ

Progression

Many successful NEBSM students use their qualifications as stepping stones to other awards, both educational and professional. Recognition is given by a number of bodies for this purpose. Further details about this and other NEBSM matters can be obtained from:

NEBSM Information Officer
The National Examining Board for Supervisory Management
76 Portland Place
London
W1N 4AA

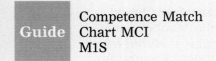

	Competence Match Chart MCI M1S

Guide — Competence Match Chart MCI M1S

The chart shows matches of Super Series 2 titles with MCI M1S (Supervisory Management) Units of Competence. Titles indicated ● are directly relevant to MCI Units, those marked ◑ provide specific supporting information, and those listed ○ provide useful general background.

NEBSM Super Series 2 Titles		1	2	3	4	5	6	7
PS1	Controlling Output	◑	◑					
PS2	Health and Safety	●	○			○		
PS3	Accident Prevention	●	○			○		
PS4	Ensuring Quality	●	○					
PS5	Quality Techniques	●						
PS6	Taking Decisions	○	○			◑	◑	
PS7	Solving Problems	○	○			◑	●	
PS8	Productivity		◑			●		
PS9	Stock Control Systems		◑					
PS10	Stores Control		◑					
PS11	Efficiency in the Office		◑			◑		
PS12	Marketing	○						
PS13	Caring for the Environment	◑	◑			○	○	○
PS14	Caring for the Customer	◑	○			○		
HR1	Supervising at Work					●	●	
HR2	Supervising with Authority					●	●	
HR3	Team Leading					●	●	
HR4	Delegation				●	●	◑	
HR5	Workteams					●	●	
HR6	Motivating People					●	●	
HR7	Leading Change		◑			●		
HR8	Personnel in Action			●				
HR9	Performance Appraisal				●		●	
HR10	Managing Time		○		○			
HR11	Hiring People			●				
HR12	Interviewing			●	●	◑	●	
HR13	Training Plans				●			
HR14	Training Sessions				●			
HR15	Industrial Relations						●	
HR16	Employment and the Law			○			●	
HR17	Equality at Work			◑			●	
HR18	Work-based Assessment			○	●	●	○	○
FR1	Accounting for Money		●					
FR2	Control via Budgets		●					
FR3	Controlling Costs		●					
FR4	Pay Systems							
FR5	Security	◑	◑					
IN1	Communicating	○	○	○	○	○	○	●
IN2	Speaking Skills	○	○	○	○	○	○	●
IN3	Orders and Instructions	◑				●	●	
IN4	Meetings				○	●	◑	●
IN5	Writing Skills	○	◑			○	◑	●
IN6	Project Preparation				○			
IN7	Using Statistics	◑	◑					●
IN8	Presenting Figures	◑	◑					●
IN9	Introduction to Information Technology	◑	◑					●
IN10	Computers and Communication Systems	◑	◑					●

MCI M1 S Units of Competence (see below*)

* **MCI M1 S Units of Competence**

1. Maintain services and operations to meet quality standards
2. Contribute to the planning, monitoring and control of resources
3. Contribute to the provision of personnel
4. Contribute to the training and development of teams, individuals and self to enhance performance
5. Contribute to the planning, organization and evaluation of work
6. Create, maintain and enhance productive working relationships
7. Provide information and advice for action towards meeting organizational objectives

The chart indicates the Super Series 2 titles which provide some useful background information to support MCI M1 (Management level 1) Units of Competence.

NEBSM Super Series 2 Titles		1	2	3	4	5	6	7	8	9
PS1	Controlling Output	△	△							
PS2	Health and Safety	△								
PS3	Accident Prevention	△								
PS4	Ensuring Quality	△	△							
PS5	Quality Techniques	△	△							
PS6	Taking Decisions								△	△
PS7	Solving Problems		△						△	△
PS8	Productivity		△							
PS9	Stock Control Systems	△								
PS10	Stores Control	△								
PS11	Efficiency in the Office	△	△							
PS12	Marketing	△								
PS13	Caring for the Environment	△								
PS14	Caring for the Customer		△							
HR1	Supervising at Work							△		
HR2	Supervising with Authority							△		△
HR3	Team Leading					△	△	△		
HR4	Delegation					△	△	△		
HR5	Workteams					△	△	△		△
HR6	Motivating People							△		
HR7	Leading Change		△							
HR8	Personnel in Action				△					
HR9	Performance Appraisal							△		
HR10	Managing Time									
HR11	Hiring People				△					
HR12	Interviewing				△	△		△		
HR13	Training Plans					△				
HR14	Training Sessions					△				
HR15	Industrial Relations							△		
HR16	Employment and the Law				△			△		
HR17	Equality at Work				△			△		
HR18	Work-based Assessment					△	△			
FR1	Accounting for Money			△						
FR2	Control via Budgets			△						
FR3	Controlling Costs			△						
FR4	Pay Systems									
FR5	Security									
IN1	Communicating							△		△
IN2	Speaking Skills		△					△		△
IN3	Orders and Instructions							△		△
IN4	Meetings							△		△
IN5	Writing Skills		△				△	△		△
IN6	Project Preparation		△				△	△		
IN7	Using Statistics						△	△	△	
IN8	Presenting Figures						△	△		△
IN9	Introduction to Information Technology								△	△
IN10	Computers and Communication Systems								△	△

* MCI M1 Units of Competence

Key Role: Manage Operations
  1. Maintain and improve service and product operations
  2. Contribute to the implementation of change in services, products and systems

Key Role: Manage Finance
  3. Recommend, monitor and control the use of resources

Key Role: Manage People
  4. Contribute to the recruitment and selection of personnel
  5. Develop teams, individuals and self to enhance performance
  6. Plan, allocate and evaluate work carried out by teams, individuals and self
  7. Create, maintain and enhance effective working relationships

Key Role: Manage Information
  8. Seek, evaluate and organise information for action
  9. Exchange information to solve problems and make decisions

Completion of this Certificate by an authorized and qualified person indicates that you have worked through all parts of this unit and completed all assessments. If you are studying this unit as part of a certificated programme, or think you may wish to in future, then completion of this Certificate is particularly important as it may be used for exemptions, credit accumulation or Accreditation of Prior Learning (APL). Full details can be obtained from NEBSM.

NEBSM
SUPER SERIES
Second Edition

PS6

Taking Decisions

. . . .

has satisfactorily completed this unit.

Name of Signatory . . . .
Position . . . .
Signature . . . .

Date . . . .

Official Stamp

Keep in touch

Pergamon Open Learning and NEBS Management are always happy to hear of your experiences of using the Super Series to help improve supervisory and managerial effectiveness. This will assist us with continuous product improvement, and novel approaches and success stories may be included in promotional information to illustrate to others what can be done.

1   NEBSM Super Series 2 study links

Here are the Super Series 2 units which link to *Taking Decisions*. You may find this useful when you are putting together your study programme but you should bear in mind that:

● each Super Series 2 unit stands alone and does not depend upon being used in conjunction with any other unit;

● Super Series 2 units can be used in any order which suits your learning needs.

SUPERVISING WITH AUTHORITY
How to identify the basis of your authority at work and make sure your authority matches the responsibility you carry.

SOLVING PROBLEMS
When problems are encountered, decisions usually have to be made. This unit sets out a level-headed, objective analytical approach to problems, so making decisions easier.

LEADING CHANGE
Change inevitably means that decisions have to be made. Understanding and managing change is vital to effective supervision. This unit should help you to implement change with minimum disruption.

TAKING DECISIONS
How are decisions made? Do intuitive decisions have a place? How can we adopt a systematic approach to taking decisions? We look at all these questions and other aspects of taking decisions in this unit.

MANAGING TIME
Pressures of time make decisions harder to make. The busy supervisor needs to be able to set aside time for careful thought, when effective decisions are demanded. This unit will help you find that time.

MOTIVATING PEOPLE
Supervisory decisions usually affect other people. To implement decisions effectively, you have to find ways of getting the whole team on your side. This unit will help you to do this.

DELEGATION
This unit will enable you to understand how to delegate effectively, a skill which is almost essential if you aren't to become overburdened by taking every decision yourself.

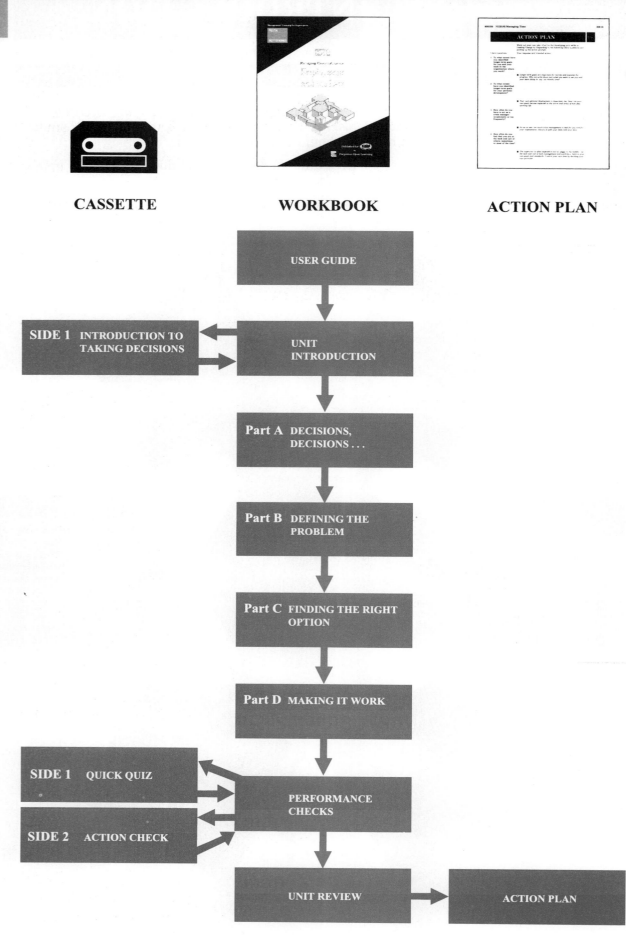

CASSETTE   WORKBOOK   ACTION PLAN

USER GUIDE

SIDE 1 INTRODUCTION TO
        TAKING DECISIONS

UNIT
INTRODUCTION

Part A DECISIONS,
        DECISIONS . . .

Part B DEFINING THE
        PROBLEM

Part C FINDING THE RIGHT
        OPTION

Part D MAKING IT WORK

SIDE 1 QUICK QUIZ

SIDE 2 ACTION CHECK

PERFORMANCE
CHECKS

UNIT REVIEW   ACTION PLAN

Supervisors are by definition leaders and decision makers.
The quality of your decisions as a supervisor is probably the
most significant factor in determining your success and that of
your team.

It's all too easy to make rash and thoughtless decisions, but less
easy to live with the consequences. In this unit we will concentrate,
therefore, on developing a strategy for thoughtful, well-informed
decisions.

Before you start work on this unit, listen carefully to Side one of the
audio cassette which sets the scene for your examination of *Taking
Decisions*.

In this unit we will:

● discuss how decisions are made;

● develop a systematic step-by-step process for making decisions;

● describe ways in which problems and desired outcomes can be
defined;

● consider how well-informed decision makers can make the best
choice between options;

● look at the implementation of decisions.

Objectives

When you have worked through this unit you will be ***better able to***:

● take a systematic, thoughtful approach to making decisions;

● understand how good and bad decisions are made;

● choose between options by careful analysis of their possible
consequences;

● implement your decisions and learn from your mistakes.

1   Introduction

The main difference that sets apart supervisors and managers from other employees is the kind and number of decisions that they make.

Some decisions are easy, some are difficult, and some may appear to be impossible!

To start this unit we look at:

● the relationship between decisions and problems;

● complex and simple decisions;

● how decisions are made;

● intuitive decisions and 'thinking' decisions.

We also set out the steps of a plan for thoughtful decision making that will serve to guide us through the remainder of the unit.

2   What's your problem?

Case Study

At the Council depot, Mark Keeley was wondering what to do. Over 20 per cent of his staff were absent this morning. How could he run a normal refuse collection service with so many people away?

On June Prebbil's line in the toy factory, work had come to a stop. The whole of the last batch of work had been rejected by the quality control department. June knew she had to get to the bottom of the problem – there was no quick and easy answer to this one. Meanwhile, her team were sitting and chatting, awaiting her instructions ...

Fazal Hussain had been called in to see the boss. Apparently there was a new rush order to complete. Fazal listened, wondering how he could juggle priorities to meet the demand, and still keep his promises to his team to cut down on the overtime they had to work.

At the supermarket bakery department, it wasn't only the heat from the ovens making Joyce feel hot under the collar. She felt she just couldn't work alongside Mavis any longer, after what she'd said. Joyce decided to take her problem to the supervisor ...

Supervisors have to deal with problems like these all the time, don't they? And of course problems nearly always involve having to make decisions:

● how to 'juggle' priorities;

● which option is the best – or the least worst;

● how to find out the true facts;

● how to keep everybody happy, and so on.

Problems and decisions seem to go hand in hand.

But do decisions always come about as a result of problems?

Part A | Activity 1

■ Time guide 3 minutes

Can you think of a decision that you wouldn't describe as involving a problem?

_____

_____

_____

As you may have observed, we all have to make fairly trivial decisions all the time. We decide what to wear, what to eat for lunch, whether or not to invite someone for a drink – in fact we all take countless decisions about things we seldom think of as problems.

This happens at work, too. If we have a clear idea of a task we want done and how we want it done, we may have no difficulty in answering a team member's queries such as: 'What shall I do now?' or 'How do I do this?' We are making decisions quickly and without the need for much conscious thought.

So at least two kinds of decisions can be identified: those which require careful conscious thought, and those which don't.

However, it's important to make the distinction between a quick decision based on knowledge and experience, and a 'thoughtless decision'.

> Decisions mostly involve making judgements, based on understanding. The better your understanding, the better chance you have of making sound judgements.

Activity 2

■ Time guide 3 minutes

If you observe someone consistently making good decisions about a complex subject *without* much apparent thought, what assumption is it reasonable to make about that person?

_____

_____

The reasonable assumption, as I hope you agree, is that the consistently good decision maker *is experienced in making those kinds of decisions*. The apparent lack of thought is misleading, because:

■ much of the thinking – and learning – has taken place in the past, when similar decisions have been made;

■ what an outsider might assume to be a new situation the experienced decision maker perceives as merely a variation of an earlier pattern of events.

For example, an experienced milkman who has to decide each morning how many bottles of milk to load on his vehicle probably won't spend long thinking about it, even though the demand from his customers may vary daily. A new person to the job might spend much longer deciding the same question.

In summing up this first section, we can say that:

• problems generally involve having to make decisions;

• only trivial decisions can be made with little thought;

• apparently effortless decisions made about complex subjects are invariably based on an experience of making similar decisions in the past.

3   How difficult are decisions?

**3.1
Complexity**

We have made a distinction between decisions requiring thought and decisions made without much thought. We might say that this was the difference between *simple* decisions and *complex* decisions.

But some decisions are more complex than others.

Activity 3

■ Time guide 6 minutes

How would you categorize each of the following situations in which your decision is required? Give each one a rating from 1 to 10, where 1 means very easy and 10 means very difficult.

Decision rating
1–10

■ You are given a choice of tea or coffee.

■ You need to decide whether to pay cash for an item or to use your credit card.

■ You have been told that one of your team must go. You now have to decide which member to make redundant.

■ You have been offered a new job in another department. You know that your team members don't want you to take it. You are torn between loyalty to your team and a desire to see the job through on the one hand, and a desire for promotion on the other.

■ Your boss has given you three important tasks to do, and has set a deadline on each one. You feel there's no one to whom you could delegate any of the tasks. Meanwhile you have to carry out your normal job of supervising. At home there are a number of matters requiring your urgent attention. Apart from all this, you haven't been feeling well and you would dearly like to take a holiday. One thing is clear: you won't manage to achieve everything. You've got to make up your mind which of these demands you will fail to respond to.

■ A new set of work procedures has been agreed, and your boss tells you that you have three months to decide how to get your team and work area organized for the changes. This is plenty of time, providing you start planning now.

There are no right or wrong answers here. The way you rated these problems depends on your own interpretation and on what sort of decisions you are used to making. For example, perhaps most people would rate the first one – the choice between tea or coffee – as a trivial decision, and give it a rating of 1. But if you don't happen to drink tea or coffee the decision may become impossible!

Let's look at the others.

■ You need to decide whether to pay cash for an item or to use your credit card.

This is a personal choice, probably affecting no one else. There may be a number of factors to think about – how much cash you have, whether you've exceeded your card credit limit and so on. My rating would be 2.

■ You have been told that one of your team must go. You now have to decide which member to make redundant.

This is a hard one, isn't it? What a terrible choice to make. No matter what you do, someone has to get bad news. I'd rate this at 9 or 10.

■ You have been offered a new job in another department. You know that your team members don't want you to take it. You are torn between loyalty to your team and a desire to see the job through on the one hand, and a desire for promotion on the other.

Again, there are others involved, but the decision probably isn't anywhere near as difficult as the previous problem. My rating would be 5 or 6.

■ Your boss has given you three important tasks to do, and has set a deadline on each one. You feel there's no one to whom you could delegate any of the tasks. Meanwhile you have to carry out your normal job of supervising. At home there are a number of matters requiring your urgent attention. Apart from all this, you haven't been feeling well and you would dearly like to take a holiday. One thing is clear: you won't manage to achieve everything. You've got to make up your mind which of these demands you will fail to respond to.

This decision is complicated by all the factors involved. Some people might feel this to be a very stressful situation and find the decision hard to make. Others might remark that it sounded like their normal day! A rating of 6 or 7 in my view.

■ A new set of work procedures has been agreed, and your boss tells you that you have three months to decide how to get your team and work area organized for the changes. This is plenty of time, providing you start planning now.

This situation looks like involving a number of decisions. However, time is on your side. Because of this, I would rate the difficulty as about 5 or 6.

Generally speaking, I would say that **decisions are harder**:

● when there are other people involved;

● the more aspects there are to consider;

● the less time there is.

Activity 4

■ Time guide 2 minutes

Would you say that it's harder to take a decision involving numbers and calculations, or one involving judgement and estimation?

_____

Perhaps you agree that decisions involving *quantities* are often easier to make than decisions involving *qualities*.
For example, if someone working at a plant nursery was given two instructions:

'Don't send out any Begonias under eight centimetres tall.'

and

'Don't send out any Begonias which look unattractive.'

the first instruction would probably involve much easier decisions than the second.

Now let's consider the process by which decisions are made.

4	How decisions are made

**4.1
Decision options**

Imagine you have been told to draw up revised rotas for your team, ready for the introduction of a new layout of the work area. This may mean splitting up pairs of people who have worked together for some time. The changes could be upsetting for all concerned.

What are your options?

Activity 5

■ Time guide 4 minutes

Either think about the problem described above, or about a typical problem which *you* might have to face, and which involves the working arrangements of your team.

Would you make such a decision entirely by yourself, or would you discuss it with others? Who else could you talk to about it?

_____

_____

_____

_____

You might discuss such a problem with all members of your team, or some of them. You might also discuss it with other supervisors, with your family, your friends or your boss.

■ You could approach some or all of these people and ask for their advice.

■ You could ask for their ideas.

■ You could even hand the problem over to them and ask for their decision.

We'll come back to the matter of team involvement in a moment.

Are there any other options?

One option, when faced with any problem, is to do nothing at all.

Activity 6

■ Time guide 3 minutes

In a work situation, is doing nothing ever an acceptable option?

_____

If others are depending on you to make a decision, doing nothing may not seem to be a realistic or acceptable option.

However, there may be times and situations when experience tells you that doing nothing is not only acceptable but is actually the best option.

For example, suppose a team member you know well has a habit of complaining about almost every aspect of the job. You know from past experience that these complaints rarely have substance, and that if you simply listen sympathetically the complaints usually vanish (inevitably to be replaced by others). If you were to react to every complaint, you would take up a lot of your valuable time, but the team member would be no happier. So you don't ignore the complaints, but for most of the time you make a conscious decision to do nothing about them.

Also, it may be wise on occasions to postpone a decision, pending further information. (We'll discuss information gathering later in the unit.)

Activity 7

> ■ Time guide 4 minutes
>
> Which of the following would you choose as the best approach to decision making for a supervisor?
>
> ■ Making all decisions personally, without reference to anyone else. ☐
>
> ■ Asking the team to vote on decisions. ☐
>
> ■ Not taking a decision until every team member has agreed to it. ☐
>
> ■ Consulting some team members, if the supervisor feels it is appropriate in the circumstances. ☐
>
> ■ Consulting all team members from time to time, but retaining the right to the last word on the subject. ☐
>
> ■ Taking an approach dependent on the people, the problem and the circumstances. ☐

You may agree with me that, if we are talking in general terms, the best answer is probably the last. The extent to which a supervisor consults his or her team should depend on the people involved, the problem to be solved, and the particular circumstances. (Notice that we even have to make decisions on how we will tackle decisions!)

Having said that, decision-making styles vary from person to person. Let's look at the two extremes.

Some supervisors like to involve their workteams in every possible decision. This 'democratic' approach can work very well for some groups, because 'being involved' is a great motivator.

However, there is a danger in taking things too far in this direction.

● For one thing, the more people who are involved in a decision, the longer it generally takes to come to an agreement.

● For another, group decisions tend to be conservative and unadventurous. Sometimes a situation calls for boldness and enterprise.

Others adopt an 'autocratic' approach – taking the line that 'I'm in charge, so I'll make all the decisions.'

This method has the advantage that, if sweeping changes are needed, one person is often able to achieve much more in a quicker time than a group would. But by not involving the team, the supervisor may be ignoring a wealth of experience and knowledge. What's more, the autocratic approach may have the effect of widening the divide between supervisor and workteam.

Generally speaking I would say that

> no one decision-making style is appropriate for all circumstances.

Part A

Activity 8

■ Time guide 4 minutes

Perhaps you can think of an occasion when a decision you made turned out to be an unwise one? Can you recall what went wrong? Jot down what you can recollect about it.

_____

_____

_____

_____

Bad or wrong decisions arise from any one of a number of things. Some of them are listed here.

● Acting impulsively – not thinking the problem through.

● Not being well enough informed – not having enough information upon which to make a sound judgement. This may be due to:

– the decision maker not making enough effort to gather together all the facts;

– the required information simply not being available;

– lack of time to collect the needed information.

● Not having a clear idea of what the decision is meant to achieve.

For instance, thinking back to the problem at the start of this section – the revised work rota – the decision depends very much on the desired outcome. One desired outcome would be to try to keep the team happy at all costs. Another might be to achieve maximum efficiency, regardless of personal feelings. Yet another might be to keep costs down to the minimum. Until you define your desired outcome, you can't make a good decision.

● Not considering all the options.

It's easy to allow personal bias to influence our decisions, or to be so concerned with one aspect, we fail to notice others.

As an example, look at the following situation.

Activity 9

■ Time guide 4 minutes

Suppose a supervisor needs to appoint a deputy to stand in for him when he's absent. The choice appears to be between two particular team members. One is better qualified and experienced than the other. However, the team seem to get along better with the less experienced member.

Jot down some of the options the supervisor has. Try to list _three_ options.

_____

_____

_____

12

There is apparently a straight choice between the two members. But our supervisor might consider:

■ giving both members a chance to do the job, on separate occasions – perhaps with the understanding that a permanent appointment is still a possibility in the future;

■ splitting the responsibility – making one member responsible for (say) the technical aspects of the job and the other for the personnel aspects;

■ appointing one member for a trial period, giving this person some help and advice in overcoming any shortcomings, and making it clear how his or her performance will be assessed;

■ not appointing a deputy immediately, but allowing *all* team members to apply for the job, stating that the appointment will be judged on both experience and personality.

There are no doubt several other possible courses of action, as you may have noted.

As we go through the unit, we will consider many of these aspects of decision making again.

5 A step-by-step guide to decision making

In the next section, we'll talk about instinctive decisions, made on the basis of intuition, rather than conscious thought.

In this section though, I want to develop a step-by-step outline for 'thinking' decisions, used for problem solving, which can guide us through the remainder of the unit.

**5.1
Preparing for
decision making**

First, a preliminary step.

As we discussed earlier, careful conscious thought is generally needed to solve problems. Only trivial decisions can be made with little thought. It follows that a decision cannot be made about a problem until it is recognized and acknowledged as a problem.

Step 1

So the first step in the process of making thinking decisions is:

acknowledgement of the problem.

Activity 10

> ■ Time guide 3 minutes
>
> Having acknowledged that a problem exists, what do you think is the next logical step to take?
>
> _____
>
> _____

I hope you agree that the most logical step is to define the problem: to express it in words. The aim is bring into focus the essential points of the matter causing the difficulty. By doing that, we should be better able to see more clearly what we may have to do to solve the problem. (It sometimes happens that this process of definition makes the problem disappear.)

Step 2

So step two is:

definition of the problem.

Activity 11

> ■ Time guide 3 minutes
>
> Having acknowledged and defined the problem, we need to look ahead to the ***outcome***. With that in mind, jot down what you think might be a good next step to make in our decision-making process.
>
> _____
>
> _____

See whether your response agrees with mine.

Thinking back to the last section, the point was made that wrong decisions are often caused by 'Not having a clear idea of what the decision is meant to achieve.'

If we put this around the other way, we might say that to make good decisions, you need to define what you want and expect from the outcome.

Step 3

An appropriate next step would therefore seem to be to set out:

our ***expectations*** of the outcome.

What next? Well, it is very rare that we are in the happy position of being entirely free to make any decision we would like to about a problem. There are always constraints: cost constraints, time constraints, efficiency constraints, and so on. Your boss may allow you only a limited authority.

For example, he or she may permit you to decide new work schedules, but not to negotiate with the Union representative about overtime.

So, having acknowledged and defined the problem, expressed our expectations of the outcome, we next need to take note of the constraints on the permissible range of options.

Step 4

This step then involves stating:

the ***constraints*** on the options.

**5.2
Making the decision**

Those are all the preliminaries out of the way. Now we can start to decide on the best course of action. Before we can do that, however, at least one more step is needed.

Activity 12

> ■ Time guide 3 minutes
>
> Can you think what else might need to be done before being able to choose a suitable option?
>
> _____
>
> _____

You may have suggested: 'Knowing what the options are.' This would be correct.

However, before listing the options, we might be in the position of having too little information in order to make a sound decision.

Step 5   So I would list Step 5 as:

information gathering.

Step 6   Once all sources of appropriate information have been exhausted, we will be at the stage of setting out our options. From these options we can finally make the decision by:

the *selection* of an option.

5.3
Putting thoughts into action

Step 7   Now we have the task of acting upon our decision, or in other words:

the *implementation* of the decision.

At the implementation stage it may become apparent that the decision was not the correct one.

> It's important to evaluate the *actual* outcome in terms of the *desired* outcome.

Step 8   With luck, it may be possible to change the decision. So Step 8 is:

outcome evaluation.

Step 9   After that, there may still be something to be learned. Other problems will arise and consequences of one decision can affect (or cause) new problems. So the final step of the decision-making process involves both looking back at what can be learned, and looking forward to solving new problems. For convenience we can express this last step briefly as:

next problem?

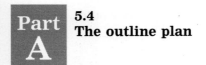

Part A

**5.4
The outline plan**

All these steps together provide our outline plan for thoughtful decision making.

As an aid to memory, the key words have been chosen so their initial letters read

'A DECISION',

as you can see in the table:

Acknowledgement of the problem
Definition of the problem
Expectations of the outcome
Constraints on the options
Information gathering
Selection of an option
Implementation of the decision
Outcome evaluation
Next problem?

In the next three parts of the unit, we'll examine all of the steps in more detail.

Before that, let's compare thinking decisions with intuitive decisions.

6   Thinking It through...

It is said that most managers and supervisors don't spend much time in deliberate conscious thought.

This doesn't of course mean that they don't think. Many supervisors spend much of their time 'thinking on their feet' – making decisions based on judgment, knowledge and experience.

But this kind of thinking can become a habit. People who spend most of their time making 'spot decisions' may tend to carry on in that vein, even when faced with difficult problems requiring deliberate, careful, systematic thought, and a need to weigh up all the options.

Activity 13

■ Time guide 3 minutes

How much of your working day is spent in careful systematic thought – as opposed to busy activities and 'thinking while working'? Make an estimate:

| 1%? | | 5%? | | 10%? | | 25%? | | 50%? | |

What prevents you from spending more time in the first kind of thinking?

_____

_____

You may well have ticked one of the first three boxes – you are probably unusual if you spend more time in deliberate systematic thought than this. In fact, you may be of the opinion that you aren't paid to think, but to act!

But, as I hope to persuade you, you can make better decisions by spending more of your time thinking problems through in a systematic way.

Your reasons for not spending more time in careful systematic thought may include:

■ having insufficient time;

■ having too many interruptions;

■ having nowhere quiet where you can think.

There is one other reason which few might admit to: thinking is difficult!

Let's look more closely at two of these reasons.

6.1 Interruptions

Perhaps the most common reason why supervisors and managers tend to spend less time than they should in deliberate thought is that their lives are full of interruptions.

You know how it is. You arrive at work with perhaps a long list in your head of the things you plan to do, and the first thing that greets you is a personnel problem, or a machine out of service, or a rush job, or any one of a hundred other kinds of problem you are expected to deal with. You may be faced with a number of decisions which have to be taken – and taken quickly – before you can get back to your original list.

Then, throughout the day, you are subjected to a steady stream of interruptions. Your boss demands an instant report. Your team members bring you their work problems, their personnel problems – perhaps even their domestic problems. You are so busy, even your interruptions are interrupted!

What's to be done about it?

One method is to set aside a period during each day when you are 'unavailable'. You let it be known that (say) for an hour starting at the same time every day is your 'thinking time' – when you tackle those problems which need careful consideration and planning.

> We don't have room in this unit to consider 'time management' any further, even though how you manage your time may have a great deal of impact on the way you make decisions.

**6.2
Thought is
hard work**

A second reason why some supervisors and managers shy away from careful thought is that it is very hard work – especially for people who aren't used to it.

Because it's usually difficult to obtain the information needed for making sound judgements, there is always a temptation to cut corners and make rash assumptions.

Most of all, if you spend the majority of your time making decisions based on experience and intuition, it's very easy to get into the habit of making *all* your decisions in this way.

We'll take a look now at decision making based on intuition. For the remainder of the unit though, we'll spend our time discussing our outline plan for thoughtful decision making.

7   ...Or relying on intuition?

It would be wrong to give the impression that decisions not involving conscious systematic thought are necessarily inefficient or ineffective.

The point has already been made that most of us make many decisions quite successfully without much conscious thought.

Many such decisions are based on *intuition*. We 'know' or 'feel' that a certain action is the right one. Or we 'sense' when a situation 'looks' right (or wrong).

Many great and famous people have demonstrated their highly developed intuition, enabling them to see the correct course of action while others were still wondering what to do.

What is intuition?

Activity 14

■ Time guide 5 minutes

Think back to a decision you've made in the past based on intuition or instinct. Write down what you can remember about it.

_____

_____

_____

_____

In hindsight, do you now think that your decision was the right one? Yes/No

Do you think that your intuitive or instinctive decision was the result of:

■ a natural 'flair' for seeing through complex situations?

| Yes | No | Perhaps |

■ previous decisions made in the same or similar situations?

| Yes | No | Perhaps |

■ information that you absorbed at the time without realizing it?

| Yes | No | Perhaps |

■ quick thinking?

| Yes | No | Perhaps |

■ logical processes that went on in your subconscious mind?

| Yes | No | Perhaps |

■ observations that you made, because you are trained to be observant in situations like this?

| Yes | No | Perhaps |

■ some other reason:

_____

_____

This is another activity where there are no correct answers. You may well have ticked 'yes' or 'perhaps' to all the points listed. Or you may have just not been able to say why you made the decision in the way that you did.

It could well be that intuitive decisions are based on subconscious thoughts and observations. We may not be able to express the ideas behind our instinctive actions – in fact if we could they would hardly be instinctive!

The real difficulty most people have with instinct and intuition is knowing when to rely on it. 'Feeling' you know the right decision to take is one thing; putting your trust in that feeling is a bigger mental step.

You may agree with me that there are no golden rules. However, you might like to think about whether you would be happy to accept the following list of tips or hints:

● if not much is at stake, you don't have much to lose in putting faith in your intuition;

● where health, safety and welfare are concerned, nothing should be left to intuition or instinct;

● it's a good idea to ask yourself whether your intuitive feelings are based on experience or on guesswork; if you aren't sure, it may be best to take a more logical approach to the problem;

● if there's time, try to back up your instinct with sound reasoning.

Self check 1

■ Time guide 10 minutes

1. Fill in the blanks in the following sentences with suitable words.

   (a) Decisions mostly involve making _____ based on understanding. The better your understanding, the better chance you have of making sound _____.

   (b) Decisions are harder

      – when other _____ are involved;

      – the more _____ there are to consider;

      – the less _____ there is.

   (c) No one decision-making _____ is appropriate for all circumstances.

   (d) It's important to evaluate the _____ outcome in terms of the _____ outcome.

2. Which of the following statements are TRUE, and which FALSE?

   (a) Problems generally involve having to make decisions. TRUE/FALSE

   (b) Apparently effortless decisions made about complex subjects are invariably based on being clever. TRUE/FALSE

   (c) Doing nothing is never an option. TRUE/FALSE

   (d) A supervisor who is too 'democratic' may sometimes find that required decisions take much longer than desired. TRUE/FALSE

3. Which *two* of the following statements are the *most* common reasons for making wrong decisions?

   (a) Acting without thought.

   (b) Not having enough information.

   (c) Having too many options and too little time.

   (d) Having too much time and too few options.

4. Briefly describe the difference between an intuitive decision and a thinking decision.

Response check 1

1. (a) Decisions mostly involve making JUDGEMENTS, based on understanding. The better your understanding, the better chance you have of making sound JUDGEMENTS.

   (b) Decisions are harder:
   - when other PEOPLE are involved;
   - the more ASPECTS there are to consider;
   - the less TIME there is.

   (c) No one decision-making STYLE is appropriate for all circumstances.

   (d) It's important to evaluate the ACTUAL outcome in terms of the DESIRED outcome.

2. (a) Problems generally involve having to make decisions. This is TRUE.

   (b) Apparently effortless decisions made about complex subjects are invariably based on being clever. This is FALSE. When someone makes difficult decisions with ease, it's usually because they are used to making decisions of that kind.

   (c) Doing nothing is never an option. This is FALSE. Sometimes doing nothing is the best option, as we discussed.

   (d) A supervisor who is too 'democratic' may sometimes find that required decisions take much longer than desired. This is TRUE.

3. The two of the four statements which reflect the most common reason for making wrong decisions are:

   (a) Acting without thought.

   (b) Not having enough information.

   The other two statements:

   (c) Having too many options and too little time.

   (d) Having too much time and too few options.

   may account for some wrong decisions, but having too many options or too much time is not necessarily a disadvantage.

4. The difference between an intuitive decision and a thinking decision is that an intuitive decision is based on 'feeling' that something is right, whereas a thinking decision is based on systematic thought processes.

   (You may have used different ways to describe the difference.)

- *Decisions* mostly involve making *judgements*, based on *understanding*. The better your understanding, the better chance you have of making sound judgements.

- Decisions are harder:

  - when other *people* are involved;

  - the more *aspects* there are to consider;

  - the less *time* there is.

- To make good decisions, you need to define what you want and expect from the *outcome*.

- No one decision-making *style* is appropriate for all circumstances.

- The steps for making good decisions can be set out as:

| Acknowledgement of the problem |
| Definition of the problem |
| Expectations of the outcome |
| Constraints on the options |
| Information gathering |
| Selection of an option |
| Implementation of the decision |
| Outcome evaluation |
| Next problem? |

DEFINING THE PROBLEM

1   Introduction

This part covers the first stage of our problem-solving, decision-making outline plan.

It involves the following steps which we need to take by way of preparation for taking decisions:

● acknowledgement of the problem;

● definition of the problem;

● expectations of the outcome;

● constraints on the options.

2   Acknowledging the problem

Our list of outline points shows that the first step in our thoughtful decision making process is

Acknowledgement of the problem
Definition of the problem
Expectations of the outcome
Constraints on the options
Information gathering
Selection of an option
Implementation of the decision
Outcome evaluation
Next problem?

Acknowledgement is a good word, because it suggests:

● *perceiving* a problem;

● *recognizing* the problem for what it is, and;

● *admitting* it exists.

Acknowledging a problem isn't always an easy thing to do.

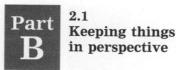

Situation 1

Imagine you are running an accounts office, dealing with 10,000 invoices a month. Suddenly your boss advises you that a new sales contract will mean that your team will have to deal with 12,000 invoices every month from now on.

Situation 2

Now imagine instead that you are running the same accounts office and over a period of time you become vaguely aware that the work is taking longer to do. It doesn't occur to you to count the number of invoices processed: if you did, you would discover that you are having to process 20 per cent more than you used to.

Activity 15

■ Time guide 2 minutes

Looking at Situations 1 and 2 above:

■ In which situation do you have a problem?

| 1 | 2 | Both |

■ In which situation is the problem acknowledged?

| 1 | 2 | Both |

The way I read it is that in both situations you have a problem, but only in Situation 1 is the problem acknowledged.

In both situations a plan for dealing with the problem is needed. However, in Situation 2 you are not sure what your problem is; until you recognize it, you have no hope of dealing with it.

This may seem a simple example. Surely, you may say, a supervisor in charge of invoice processing would be aware of the numbers processed each month? But when your life is spent organizing people and dealing with individual small queries, it's quite possible to lose sight of the overall picture.

Beware of becoming so concerned about small problems that you lose sight of the big ones.

24

Activity 16

■ Time guide 3 minutes

How can a supervisor anticipate problems? Think about your own job and a particular problem you've encountered recently. Jot down the signs that warned you (or should have warned you, looking back on things) that the problem was likely to occur.

_____

_____

_____

_____

Depending on the kind of work you do, there may be any number of signs of an impending problem, including:

■ team members behaving out of character;

■ a machine making an unusual noise;

■ a process varying more than usual;

■ inconsistent performance for no apparent reason;

■ management reorganizations;

■ a change of function or objectives;

■ a cycle of events which has lead to problems on previous occasions;

■ a change of personnel.

In fact, a change of any kind, or a recognized pattern of events or behaviour, may indicate that problems are looming. The wise supervisor is always:

● monitoring;

● observing;

● comparing;

● listening;

● looking ahead.

The next step on our list is an expression or

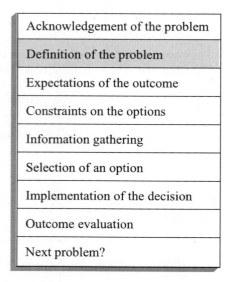

Acknowledgement of the problem
Definition of the problem
Expectations of the outcome
Constraints on the options
Information gathering
Selection of an option
Implementation of the decision
Outcome evaluation
Next problem?

This definition is best expressed in words – either by writing it down or by discussing it with someone.

Activity 17

■ Time guide 3 minutes

Do you agree that expressing a problem in words is an aid in solving the problem? | Yes | No |

Express the reason for your answer in words!

_____

_____

_____

Expressing a problem often helps, in my view. In fact, when this step is carried out, many problems either disappear, or their solution becomes immediately obvious.

**3.1
Writing It down**

If you are in the habit of writing things down, then a constructive step is to start with a blank sheet of paper and the heading:

'What is this problem?'

Other useful questions include the following.

● When did the problem begin?

● Who is involved?

● Is it my problem or someone else's?

● What are the known facts?

Notes and observations need not be set out in an orderly fashion. We aren't all natural note-takers. But just the act of writing things down can help, because expressing thoughts can help to turn vague ideas into concrete plans.

3.2
Talking It over

Talking the problem over is often very beneficial, too. The person you talk with doesn't necessarily need to be able to fully understand the technicalities – in fact the only essential requirement is that he or she is willing to listen attentively.

Part
B

Talking it over enables you to express the matter in your own terms. In doing so, you may well see deficiencies in your grasp of the problem before your audience does.

> Make a habit of expressing your problems in words.

---

4   Knowing what you want

Now we're at the third step in our process:

Acknowledgement of the problem
Definition of the problem
Expectations of the outcome
Constraints on the options
Information gathering
Selection of an option
Implementation of the decision
Outcome evaluation
Next problem?

As I think we've agreed, if a decision is to be effective, the decision maker must be clear about the desired outcome.

As an example of the way that the effects of decisions depend on the desired outcome, let's turn to the subject of disciplining someone at work.

Activity 18

■ Time guide 4 minutes

Suppose you have to discipline a member of your team for being repeatedly late for work. You call the member in for a disciplinary interview.

■ What are your objectives in holding the interview?

_____

_____

_____

■ What is your desired outcome in a case like this?

_____

_____

_____

■ Your objectives may be to discover the reasons for the persistent lateness and to warn the offender of the action that might be taken if the state of affairs continues.

■ An appropriate 'desired outcome' might be that the team member is never late again.

Yet, if they are honest, many supervisors might go into a disciplinary interview thinking one of the following.

● 'This person must be punished for such behaviour.'

● 'I must discipline this offender as an example to the others.'

● 'If I stick to the disciplinary rules, my boss is bound to approve of my actions.'

> The decisions you make depend on the outcome you are aiming for.

Step 4 on our list is:

Acknowledgement of the problem
Definition of the problem
Expectations of the outcome
Constraints on the options
Information gathering
Selection of an option
Implementation of the decision
Outcome evaluation
Next problem?

By 'constraints' I mean the limitations or controls which restrict the number of options we have. One common constraint is lack of time.

Activity 19

■ Time guide 3 minutes

Can you think of *two* other typical constraints which might be placed on you when making a decision at work, restricting your choice of options?

_____

_____

You might have mentioned some of the following constraints.

■ The requirements or demands of the boss.

 When outlining a task, your boss may insist that you comply with certain conditions.

■ The requirements or demands of the workteam.

 For example, when given an instruction to find ways of cutting running costs, you may decide to rule out recommending a reduction in staff numbers.

■ Not being able to find all the information you need.

■ Lack of resources.

■ Restraints of authority.

 Few people have unlimited authority, even within their own work area.

■ Cost constraints.

 These are perhaps the most common constraints.

■ Constraints due to limitations of your own ability.

 We all have our limitations!

■ Physical restraints.

 Such as having to operate within a limited work area.

Part
B

In addition, you may be constrained by your own conscience or beliefs.

Often, many of the different demands and requirements being made upon the supervisor are **conflicting**.

Activity 20

■ Time guide 4 minutes

Jot down **three** or **four** requirements or demands on you which often conflict, within your own work situation.

_____

_____

_____

_____

Case
Study

Here's an example of a typical situation.

A workteam is on a production bonus, which means they receive extra pay for producing more than a standard number of items. However, rejected items don't count, so they have to keep the quality up, too. At the same time, the safety officer has issued instructions about safety procedures, which limit the speed at which the team can work. Other factors, such as the supply of parts, are outside the supervisor's control. The process depends on good relations with other teams, so the supervisor spends much of her time in liaison work, whereas her team would prefer that she spent more time on dealing with their problems. Her boss demands to be kept informed of progress and all significant events, so the supervisor's time is not her own . . .

Although your work situation may be different, it is likely that you will be subject to just as many conflicting constraints.

That's what being a supervisor is all about: using your skills and judgement to cope with the many conflicting demands.

> Making decisions usually means making compromises. Few decisions leave all parties feeling completely satisfied with the outcome.

■ Time guide 5 minutes

1. Fill in the blanks in the following sentences with suitable words.

   (a) Beware of becoming so concerned about _____ problems that you lose sight of the big ones.

   (b) Make a habit of _____ your problems in words.

   (c) The decisions you make depend on the _____ you are aiming for.

   (d) Making decisions usually means making _____. Few decisions leave all parties feeling completely _____ with the outcome.

2. Which of the following statements are TRUE, and which FALSE?

   (a) A supervisor can anticipate problems by being observant. TRUE/FALSE

   (b) Writing a problem down is not as helpful as talking it over with someone. TRUE/FALSE

   (c) Supervisors are often constrained by lack of resources, but should not be constrained by the demands of the workteam. TRUE/FALSE

   (d) When the boss says 'You have a completely free hand', it means there will be absolutely no constraints on the decision you make. TRUE/FALSE

Response check 2

1. (a) Beware of becoming so concerned about SMALL problems that you lose sight of the big ones.

   (b) Make a habit of EXPRESSING your problems in words.

   (c) The decisions you make depend on the OUTCOME you are aiming for.

   (d) Making decisions usually means making COMPROMISES. Few decisions leave all parties feeling completely SATISFIED with the outcome.

2. (a) A supervisor can anticipate problems by being observant. This is TRUE.

   (b) Writing a problem down is not as helpful as talking it over with someone. This is FALSE: it is less important *how* the problem is expressed, as long as it *is* expressed.

   (c) Supervisors are often constrained by lack of resources, but should not be constrained by the demands of the workteam. This is FALSE: the demands of the workteam can sometimes be the most important aspect of a problem.

   (d) When the boss says 'You have a completely free hand', it means there will be absolutely no constraints on the decision you make. This may appear to be true, but I wonder whether you agree with me that it is a very rare problem indeed that places *no* constraints on the decision to be made, whatever the boss or anyone else says about it. I would say the statement was FALSE.

- The wise supervisor is always monitoring, observing, comparing, listening and *looking ahead for problems*.

- Problems should be *expressed in words*.

- The decisions you make depend on the *outcome you are aiming for*.

- Often, many of the different demands and requirements being made upon the supervisor are *conflicting*.

FINDING THE RIGHT OPTION

1   Introduction

Having defined the problem, there are more important activities before the choice is made:

- collecting information and ideas – from wherever and whomever they are available;

- listing the alternatives;

- looking ahead, to see what the effects of each alternative option might be.

Then at last our decision can be made.

2   Collecting information and ideas

We come now to one of the most time-consuming and (often) difficult steps:

Acknowledgement of the problem
Definition of the problem
Expectations of the outcome
Constraints on the options
Information gathering
Selection of an option
Implementation of the decision
Outcome evaluation
Next problem?

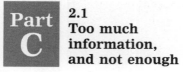

Part C

**2.1
Too much
information,
and not enough**

At times you may feel that you have more information than you can
cope with.

Activity 21

■ Time guide 4 minutes

How many sources of information are you expected to handle during your working day?

■ Facts and opinions by word of mouth from your boss, your team and your colleagues – not all of which agree. ☐

■ Written reports containing information which you are expected to absorb. ☐

■ Statistics in the form of charts and diagrams. ☐

■ Messages on written memos. ☐

■ Warnings and cautions on posters. ☐

■ Videos which are part of your training and which you have to watch. ☐

■ Other information sources. ☐

You can perhaps consider yourself lucky if you do not have to deal
with information from a great many sources, of which the list above
are typical examples.

And yet, even though you may feel sometimes that it is difficult to
cope with this deluge, the information itself is probably by no means
all relevant or useful: your biggest job may be sorting the 'wheat
from the chaff'.

It is a common experience to find that, when faced with difficult
decisions, there is a distinct lack of pertinent and helpful
information. I would go so far as to say that

> most decisions at work have to be
> made with imperfect information.

**2.2
Seeking out
information**

Nevertheless, decision makers have to do their best to get all the
relevant information they can, in the time available.

Activity 22

■ Time guide 4 minutes

What sources of information are available to you? List at least *three*.

_____

_____

_____

_____

You may have listed some of the information sources we mentioned in the previous activity. Let's look at the information sources typically available to a supervisor.

■ The workteam

For many problems, the workteam is the best informed group of people around. This is especially true when it comes to specific work problems. After all, the team members are often the people who have to deal with the problems first hand.

■ The boss

The supervisor's immediate superior is of course a good source of information, particularly on tasks that he or she has assigned. A good boss will normally be happy to supply all the information available.

■ Other supervisors

Colleagues are frequently faced with the same or similar problems. Establishing good relations with other supervisors, and encouraging a free exchange of information, can help to overcome problems of all kinds.

■ Company documents

These include such publications as the organization rule book, the health and safety policy document, technical drawings, suppliers' lists and brochures, etc.

■ Company experts

Don't forget that most organizations have departments and people part of whose function it is to provide a specialized service to other employees. These include the personnel department (for all matters affecting employment); the safety officer; the legal department (in larger companies); the computer or information technology department; the drawing office; the publications department.

■ Libraries

If your organization does not have a library, there is always the public library!

■ Official publications

There are numerous official publications, including British Standards, and the many thousands of books and papers published by HM Stationery Office. Your local library should be able to help you with these.

■ Computer databases

These are now becoming very commonly available. If your organization does not subscribe to a commercial database, your local library might.

The following diagram illustrates these typical sources of information.

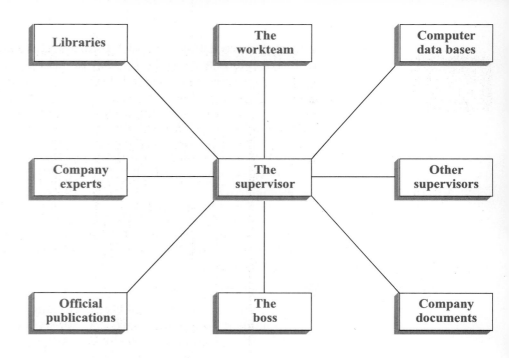

2.3
Getting ideas

Sometimes facts are not enough to solve a problem. With some problems you need a new slant on things, a fresh approach.

Thomas worked for a chain of specialist tea and coffee suppliers whose customers included both large companies and individuals. Thomas's employers were always on the look-out for new schemes for promoting products and encouraged their employees to put forward ideas. Thomas had already thought up outline plans for two promotional offers which had been adopted successfully by the company.

When tackling some problems, although a certain amount of background information may be needed, the main task is the generation of ideas. With others, you may become trapped in narrow ways of thinking; what is needed is a new way of looking at the problem.

The following approaches to generating ideas may be of help.

● Stand back from the problem.

The closer you are to a problem, the harder it is to see it from a new perspective. This is especially true if you've tried unsuccessfully to solve a similar problem in the past.

● Approach the problem with an open mind.

Explore all angles. Don't dismiss any idea until you've got the one that works best. Suspend judgement.

● Try changing the starting point.

If you tackle your problems in the same way each time, you may be stifling your own inventiveness.

● Try switching your focus of attention away from the main issue.

We tend to concentrate on the most obvious points of a problem, as the following case incident illustrates.

Case Study

Part C

A certain company was becoming concerned about the high accident rates in one of its factories. A new safety officer was appointed and he carried out a thorough inspection. On his recommendation, a great deal of money was spent on safety equipment and on a 'safety awareness' campaign. Things improved, but the accident rates were still higher than the industry norm. What the company had overlooked was that the operators were persistently trying to cut corners on safety because they were being paid high bonuses for production.

● Question everything – keep on asking 'why?'

There is a natural tendency, in all walks of life, to assume that there is a sensible, well thought out reason for everything. But if you ask the question 'Why do you do things in this way?' it's surprising how often the only answer anyone can think of is: 'Well, we always have!'

● Allow your subconscious to work for you.

The human mind is a very powerful engine. It works at more than one level. Concentrating on a problem at the conscious level doesn't always provide the solution. If you're getting nowhere, there's a lot to be said for setting a problem aside and letting the subconscious get to work. 'Sleep on it!' is often very good advice.

● Be prepared to take risks.

Some problems need a bold approach. Experiment a little. But remember – if you take risks, you need to be prepared for the worst possible outcome!

Extension 1 J. Adair, in his book *Effective Decision-Making* discusses imaginative thinking, and distinguishes between 'visualizing', 'creating', 'fantasy' and so on. This is a very interesting book to read, and is a good source of information and tips on all aspects of decision making.

---

3   Sorting out the options

Provided all our searching for information and ideas has been successful, we should be left with one or more options, or alternative solutions. We have listed this stage as:

Acknowledgement of the problem
Definition of the problem
Expectations of the outcome
Constraints on the options
Information gathering
Selection of an option
Implementation of the decision
Outcome evaluation
Next problem?

There are really three tasks involved here:

● listing the alternatives;

● looking ahead, to see what the effects of each alternative option might be;

● making a choice.

**3.1
Listing all
the alternatives**

After investigating a particular problem, most people tend to home in quickly on one or perhaps two possible solutions. However, it's a mistake to dismiss any option prematurely.

Try the following problem, which shows the advantage of not eliminating options before the consequences have been thought through.

Activity 23

■ Time guide 6 minutes

Imagine you are a supervisor at a soap factory, in charge of packing bars of luxury toilet soap. Each bar is individually wrapped by hand, using plastic film, before being put in boxes. Your problems are as follows:

■ there is limited space available for the packing work at the factory;

■ it is difficult to get enough staff to do the work, partly because the factory is on the edge of a country town where there is poor public transport, and partly because the wages are not very attractive – the firm says it cannot afford to pay more.

You are asked to come up with ideas for overcoming one or both of these problems.

What can you suggest? Try to think of *two* ideas.

_____

_____

_____

_____

You may have suggested any number of things. I'll list my ideas and ask you to choose which options look more likely to be successful.

Activity 24

■ Time guide 5 minutes

Here are my suggestions for overcoming the problems in the previous activity. Tick the one which seems the most practical and sensible of the six:

(a) renting or buying a new building to provide more room to do the packing, preferably situated nearer the centre of the town, or near the housing estates, so that it is easier for people to get to;

(b) providing a bus service to collect employees from their homes;

(c) providing higher wages to entice more people to do the work; (The firm says it cannot afford to pay higher wages, but can they afford *not* to?)

(d) sending all the packing to a subcontractor;

(e) taking the unpacked soap and packing materials to the homes of part-time employees, so that people who can neither work full-time nor travel can do the work at home in their own time;

(f) packing the soap by machine, instead of by hand.

What conclusions did you come to? In fact, in an actual case, the last two ideas were initially ruled out as being unworkable. Eventually, however, all the others were eliminated and the firm tried out option (e): it worked very well. The firm now has also made provisional plans for using machines to pack the soap.

**3.2
What happens if . . .**

Having listed all the alternatives, how can we choose between them?

For a major project involving decisions between expensive options, it may be considered worthwhile to carry out a *feasibility study*.

A feasibility study is a brief investigation to find out:

● whether a proposal is realizable;

● whether it is likely to meet all the requirements;

● what 'knock-on effects' it might have.

Often, there are three main aspects to consider.

● *Technical* feasibility

   This is intended to cover the practical aspects of (say) whether a particular machine is suited to a particular job.

● *Social* feasibility

   This considers the impact on the people involved.

● *Economic* feasibility

   This sets out to estimate to what extent financial costs are balanced by financial gains.

A fourth aspect which may come into play is the *environmental* impact of a decision – the effects on the world around us.

Part C

Activity 25

■ Time guide 5 minutes

Suppose a company has commissioned a study to look into the feasibility of introducing computer technology.

The technical feasibility part of the study would look into such questions as what equipment is needed and to what extent computers would help to speed up the company's operations.

The economic feasibility part of the study would try to determine how much money the company would save, considering both set-up costs and running costs.

What sort of questions would the company want answered on the social aspects of the study? Try to suggest *two* questions.

_____

_____

_____

_____

The questions might include the following.

■ What will be the effects on staffing numbers?

■ What training will be needed?

■ What new work-patterns will be needed?

■ How can any resistance to the proposed changes be overcome?

Where a smaller-scale project is concerned, a feasibility study may not be viable. Nevertheless, *the same kind of questions have to be answered*.

● What effect will the decision have on people?

● What is the impact of the technology?

● What effect will the decision have on costs and profits?

● What impact will the decision have on the world around us?

4	Making a choice

If you have taken time and trouble over:

● expressing the problem;

● deciding what you want and expect from the outcome;

● collecting information and ideas;

● setting out your options;

the actual step of taking the decision will often turn out to be comparatively painless.

If it is still difficult to come to a decision, it may be because you are in the happy position of having more than one attractive option – or alternatively that there are *no* attractive options.

Activity 26

■ Time guide 3 minutes

If you've followed through our step-by-step decision-making procedure, and yet still find it difficult to make a choice, it may be the time to ask some searching questions, such as:

'Have I listed all the possible options?'

Try to suggest *two* further questions you might ask yourself at this stage.

_____

_____

_____

Some questions you could ask are given below:

■ have I listed all possible options?

■ do I know enough about the effects of these options?

■ which option is most likely to provide my desired outcome?

■ has the problem changed as a result of my investigations and increased knowledge?

■ would it help to express the problem differently?

■ do I need more information?

■ do I need more ideas?

■ do I need help from others affected by the decision?

■ have I really kept an open mind, or did I have one option in mind all along, which has now turned out to be less attractive?

■ could more than one option be chosen, or a compromise between them?

> One approach, if you are still unable to decide between alternative solutions to a problem, is deliberately to set up an argument. Get a friend or colleague to champion one option, while you argue for another. The idea is for each person to try to persuade the other of the value of the option he or she 'owns'. This may bring out weaknesses and strengths not appreciated before.

■ Time guide 10 minutes

1. Which of the following statements are TRUE, and which FALSE?

    (a) Most decisions have to be made with imperfect information, so it's probably not worth spending too much time trying to collect it. TRUE/FALSE

    (b) The workteam is often one of the best sources of information for the supervisor. TRUE/FALSE

    (c) A supervisor in a typical organization has at hand many people and many documents, ready to provide information for making decisions. TRUE/FALSE

    (d) The closer you are to a problem, the easier it often is to see it from a new perspective. TRUE/FALSE

2. Which *two* of the following are the *best* ways of generating ideas to solve a problem?

    (a) Change your starting point, and tackle it from a new approach.

    (b) Concentrate on the detail.

    (c) Work at it, going over the same steps time and again, until you see the light.

    (d) Keep asking 'Why?'

3. Describe what a feasibility study is in your own words.

    _____

    _____

    _____

4. Classify each of the following questions into *one* of four categories:

    SOCIAL, TECHNICAL, ECONOMIC, ENVIRONMENTAL.

    As a result of this decision:

    (a) Will anyone have to change jobs? _____

    (b) Will running costs increase or decrease? _____

    (c) Will extra pollution be introduced? _____

    (d) Will the machines cope with the workload? _____

    (e) How much training will be required? _____

    (f) Will it increase our profits? _____

Response check 3

1. (a) Most decisions have to be made with imperfect information, so it's probably not worth spending too much time trying to collect it. This is FALSE: if you want to make the best possible decision, it's important to collect as much information as you can.

   (b) The workteam is often one the best sources of information for the supervisor. This is TRUE.

   (c) A supervisor in a typical organization has at hand many people and many documents, ready to provide information for making decisions. This is TRUE.

   (d) The closer you are to a problem, the easier it often is to see it from a new perspective. This is FALSE: getting too close to a problem can prevent you seeing it from a new perspective.

2. The best two options listed are:

   (a) Change your starting point, and tackle it from a new approach.

   (d) Keep asking 'Why?'

   Of the other two:

   (b) Concentrate on the detail.

   is not likely to help generate ideas, because it's easy to lose sight of the overall picture.

   (c) Work at it, going over the same steps time and again, until you see the light.

   may get you to the solution in the long run, but setting the problem aside for a while may bring quicker results.

3. A feasibility study is a brief investigation to find out:

   ● whether a proposal is realizable;

   ● whether it is likely to meet all the requirements, and;

   ● what 'knock-on effects' it might have.

4. I would classify the questions as follows:

   (a) Will anyone have to change jobs? SOCIAL

   (b) Will running costs increase or decrease? ECONOMIC

   (c) Will extra pollution be introduced? ENVIRONMENTAL

   (d) Will the machines cope with the workload? TECHNICAL

   (e) How much training will be required? SOCIAL

   (f) Will it increase our profits? ECONOMIC

● Most decisions at work have to be made with *imperfect information*. The best decision makers are the best informed ones.

● Typical sources of information for the supervisor are:

   – the workteam;

   – the boss;

   – other supervisors;

   – company documents;

   – company experts;

   – libraries;

   – official publications;

   – computer databases.

● Selecting an option involves:

   – listing the alternatives;

   – looking ahead, to see what the effects of each alternative option might be, and finally;

   – making a choice.

● Decisions of all kinds may entail asking the following questions.

   – What effect will the decision have on people?

   – What is the impact of the technology?

   – What effect will the decision have on costs and profits?

   – What impact will the decision have on the world around us?

MAKING IT WORK

1   Introduction

Once our decision is finally made, it has to be put into effect.

Will it survive contact with reality? Have we been making incorrect assumptions? Have we allowed for all contingencies?

After giving the decision all the thought and attention we have time for, sooner or later we have to stop thinking and start acting.

In this part, we'll look at:

● implementing a decision;

● assessing the outcome;

● looking back to see what can be learned;

● looking forward to the next problem.

2   Implementation

Now we arrive at the point where the decision has to be put into effect. In other words:

Acknowledgement of the problem
Definition of the problem
Expectations of the outcome
Constraints on the options
Information gathering
Selection of an option
Implementation of the decision
Outcome evaluation
Next problem?

Part D

2.1
Getting things done

The successful implementation of decisions requires people who can 'get things done'.

Activity 27

■ Time guide 6 minutes

Which of the following would you say are typical characteristics of a person who is an 'achiever' – someone who 'gets things done' at work?

(a) The ability to establish clear goals and to keep them firmly in mind.

(b) The doggedness to forge on without clear objectives.

(c) The independence to ignore offers of help from others.

(d) The willingness to accept help from others provided this help is directed towards the defined objectives.

(e) The courage to take risks.

(f) The sense not to take risks.

(g) The perseverance to pursue an objective until it is achieved.

(h) The sense of proportion which prevents pursuit of evasive goals.

(i) The total belief in oneself and a refusal to acknowledge that mistakes are possible.

(j) The humility to admit mistakes and to try to learn from them.

(k) The willingness to learn from the experiences of others.

(l) The ability to realize that to tread new paths it is necessary to 're-invent the wheel'.

You may have found that this Activity required some thought. My response is that (a), (d), (e), (g), (j) and (k) are the characteristics typical of an 'achiever'.

Let's review those points again.

- ◼ The ability to establish clear goals and to keep them firmly in mind.

  This is very important. You can see people all the time who work hard, but make little progress owing either to having no clear goals, or having lost sight of their goals.

- ◼ The willingness to accept help from others provided this help is directed towards the defined objectives.

  Being too independent is usually a fault, in my view. Achievement at work is a team effort. While individual achievement is to be applauded for itself, working on your own makes the job much tougher.

- ◼ The courage to take risks.

  Timid people are not renowned for their achievements. Boldness is needed to get things done.

- ◼ The perseverance to pursue an objective until it is achieved.

  Tenacity and single-mindedness are characteristics which separate the achiever from the non-achiever.

- ◼ The humility to admit mistakes and to try to learn from them.

  Belief in oneself is very desirable but not if it extends to a refusal to admit one's mistakes.

- ◼ The willingness to learn from the experiences of others.

  There is no point in treading new paths if the correct path has already been discovered.

You will notice that by following our step-by-step decision-making process:

- ● objectives are defined;

- ● the decision maker (and implementer) is armed with knowledge about the subject;

- ● the help of others has already been called upon to gain information and ideas, so that it should be a natural progression to involving these people in the implementation of the decision.

2.2
The acid test:
will it work?

No matter how much time has been spent in preparing for a decision, it doesn't always follow that the choice made was the correct one.

It's always possible that a vital point has been overlooked, or the importance of some aspect has been underestimated.

A common mistake is to misjudge the reaction of the people affected by the decision, as the following case incident illustrates.

Case
Study

Monty Farr had agonized over the decision of whom to appoint to the position of supervisor of the maintenance night-shift. He had eventually chosen Gilbert Dodwell. He knew Gilbert was keen and ambitious, and it should be possible to overcome the man's lack of experience, provided he was given help and support. Gilbert had been disappointed to be turned down for an earlier appointment. Monty provisionally made up his mind on Friday, thought about it all weekend, and came to a final decision on Monday morning. He was ready for any complaints from two of his more experienced people whom he had also considered for the job. Monty had also worked out detailed plans, so that there would be minimum disruption when Gilbert switched from one job to another. So far as he could tell, he'd thought about all aspects of the decision. All that was left to be done was to tell Gilbert the good news.

When he did tell him, Monty was extremely surprised to hear Gilbert turn the job down without a moment's hesitation. 'Thanks for the offer, Monty, but it's impossible,' Gilbert said. 'I just could not contemplate working a permanent night shift.'

Activity 28

■ Time guide 3 minutes

In the case above, you might say Monty was not well enough informed to make a good decision. How could he have avoided having his offer turned down?

_____

_____

_____

Perhaps you agree that, where people are going to be affected by a decision, it's best, if possible, to consult them in advance. In this case, it might have been more sensible for Monty to ask for volunteers for the job first. Just because somebody is keen and ambitious, it doesn't mean to say that they'll take any promotion offered.

It's easy to misjudge a situation, and we all make unwise decisions from time to time. When it happens, we have to think again. What is important is to learn from the experience.

The next step is:

Acknowledgement of the problem
Definition of the problem
Expectations of the outcome
Constraints on the options
Information gathering
Selection of an option
Implementation of the decision
Outcome evaluation
Next problem?

In the first section of the unit, we said that

> it's important to evaluate the *actual* outcome in terms of the *desired* outcome.

In other words, having put your decision into effect, you need to ask such questions as the following.

● Have my objectives been achieved?

● What are the reactions to the decision by those affected by it?

Activity 29

■ **Time guide 3 minutes**

Can you think of any more questions which it would seem sensible to ask at this stage, and which would help us to evaluate a decision? Try to note *two* more questions if you can.
(Hint: read through the steps of our step-by-step process again.)

_____

_____

_____

Other relevant questions are listed here.

■ Has the decision made about this problem caused any new problems?

■ Did my definition of the original problem prove to be correct?

■ Did I meet all the constraints?

■ Did the information I gathered prove to be sufficient to make a good decision?

■ Is the outcome acceptable to all involved?

■ Have all my desired outcomes been achieved?

Perhaps the most searching question is:

■ In the same circumstances, would I make the same decision again?

---

4   Looking back – and forward

Finally, we have reached the last step in our process:

Acknowledgement of the problem
Definition of the problem
Expectations of the outcome
Constraints on the options
Information gathering
Selection of an option
Implementation of the decision
Outcome evaluation
Next problem?

This is the stage when we need to:

● **look back** – to see what we have learned;

● **look forward** – to see how this decision can help with the next.

Some questions to be asked are listed here.

● What was the cause of the original problem? Could it have been avoided? Could it have been dealt with in a different way? Was the problem correctly recognized?

● Did I spot the problem early enough?

● Was my approach to the problem the best one, now that I look back over it?

● What have I learned?

● Did I identify all possible options?

● Should I modify my decision-making techniques?

● How can my work on this problem help me tackle new problems?

Remember that:

> - the better you know your job, the easier the decisions become;
>
> - the better you know your team, the easier the decisions become;
>
> - the better you know how your organization works, the easier the decisions become;
>
> - the more decisions you make, the easier the decisions become.

Self check 4

■ Time guide 5 minutes

1. Which of the following statements are TRUE, and which FALSE?

   The typical 'achiever':

   (a) depends on other people to get things done. TRUE/FALSE

   (b) is willing to learn from the mistakes other people make. TRUE/FALSE

   (c) is dogged and persevering. TRUE/FALSE

   (d) takes risks by making decisions before finding out the facts. TRUE/FALSE

2. Fill in the blanks in the table with suitable words:

_____ of the problem
Definition of the _____
_____ of the outcome
Constraints on the options
_____ gathering
Selection of an _____
Implementation of the decision
_____ evaluation
Next problem?

51

Response check 4

1. The typical 'achiever':

   (a) depends on other people to get things done. This is both TRUE and FALSE! The achiever in a work situation inevitably does rely on others to help him or her, because most employees are part of a group or team. But the real achiever will accomplish things in spite of hindrance from others.

   (b) is willing to learn from the mistakes other people make. This is TRUE.

   (c) is dogged and persevering. This is TRUE.

   (d) takes risks by making decisions before finding out the facts. This is FALSE: it is folly to take this kind of risk; the achiever is not a foolish person.

2.

ACKNOWLEDGEMENT of the problem
Definition of the PROBLEM
EXPECTATIONS of the outcome
Constraints on the options
INFORMATION gathering
Selection of an OPTION
Implementation of the decision
OUTCOME evaluation
Next problem?

5   Summary

- Someone who is an 'achiever' will:
  - keep goals firmly in mind;
  - accept the help of others;
  - take risks;
  - persevere;
  - learn from mistakes.
- No one makes good decisions all the time. The clever people don't make the same mistake twice.
- It's important to evaluate the *actual* outcome in terms of the *desired* outcome.
- Decisions become easier:
  - the better you know your job, your team and your organization;
  - the more decisions you make.

PERFORMANCE CHECKS

1	Quick quiz

Well done – you have completed the unit. Now listen to the questions on Side one of the audio cassette. If you are not sure about some of the answers, check back in the workbook before making up your mind.

Write down your answers in the space below.

1 _____

_____

2 _____

_____

3 _____

_____

4 _____

_____

5 _____

_____

6 _____

_____

7 _____

_____

8 _____

_____

9 _____

_____

10 _____

_____

11 _____

_____

12 _____

_____

13 _____

_____

14 _____

_____

15 _____

_____

2   Action check

On Side two of the audio cassette, you will hear some discussions about taking decisions.

Listen carefully to the extracts, and try to answer the questions.

Write your answers and comments in the space below.

Situation 1:

_____

_____

_____

_____

_____

_____

Situation 2:

_____

_____

_____

_____

_____

_____

Situation 3:

_____

_____

_____

_____

_____

_____

Situation 4: _____

_____

_____

_____

_____

_____

3   Unit assessment

Time guide 60 minutes

Case Study

Read the following case incident and then deal with the questions which follow, writing your answers on a separate sheet of paper.

Lettie Manning is supervisor to a workteam of 15 people in a supermarket distribution warehouse.

A two-shift system is in operation: the first shift runs from 7 a.m. to 2 p.m., and the second from 1 p.m. to 8 p.m.

The team's main task is to pack food items for distribution to a chain of supermarkets. Conveyor belts are used to move the goods from the storage area to the outgoing collection areas. The team's normal throughput rate is around 10,000 items an hour. With breaks for meals etc., the line runs for 12 hours a day.

Lettie's manager arrives one Friday afternoon and tells her that, when two new supermarket branches are opened in a month's time, it is estimated that the warehouse will need to ship 150,000 items a day.

Lettie is asked to make plans to deal with this increase in throughput rate. Any options will be considered, but as usual, cost will be a major consideration.

You need only write *one* or *two* sentences in reply to each question.

1. What problems might Lettie foresee as a result of this change?

2. What decisions will Lettie have to make in putting forward her proposals?

3. What are the constraints on these decisions?

4. How can Lettie best define the desired outcome of these decisions?

5. What further information might you require if you were making these decisions yourself?

6. From the description above, what would you say were Lettie's best options?

55

Time guide 60 minutes

The time guide for this assignment gives you an approximate idea of how long it is likely to take you to write up your findings.

You will need to spend some additional time gathering information, perhaps talking to colleagues and thinking about the assignment. The result of your efforts should be presented on separate sheets of paper.

1. List ***three*** important decisions you have had to make recently during the course of your work.

   For each decision, explain:

   (a) your approach to making the decision;

   (b) how successful the decision turned out to be;

   (c) what you would have done differently, looking back.

2. Using our chart (reproduced below) as a starting point, draw up your own personal reference list of information sources. Be as specific as you can. For instance, if your organization has a personnel department, talk to someone about the ways in which the people in that department can help you with personnel problems.

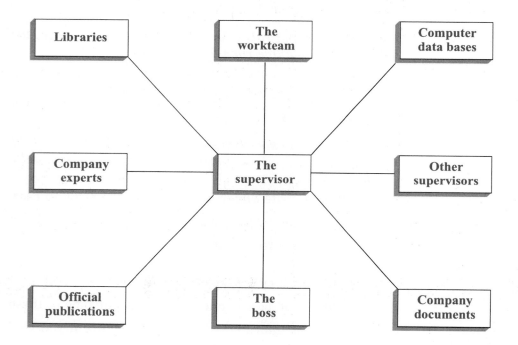

UNIT REVIEW

1 Return to objectives

Now that you have completed your work on this unit, let's review each of our unit objectives.

You will be **better able to**:

● take a systematic, thoughtful approach to making decisions;

Our step-by-step process for good decision making is designed to help you think about the important decisions you have to make and to approach them in a systematic way. Because most decisions at work are based on inadequate information, it is well worth spending time and effort in making use of all the information sources available.

● understand how good and bad decisions are made;

As we discussed, incorrect decisions come about mainly through inadequate information, rash assumptions and through mistaking guesswork for 'inspired intuition'. Good decisions on the other hand are based on thought, experience and knowledge.

● choose between options by careful analysis of their possible consequences;

The good decision maker thinks not only about the immediate consequences of an action, but of the 'knock on' effects. By analyzing possible reactions and repercussions, options can be compared and the best one chosen.

● implement your decisions and learn from your mistakes.

At the implementation stage, your attention must turn from the decision process itself to ensuring that the decision is successfully put into effect. The person who 'gets things done' is someone who has clear goals, is unwavering in pursuit of those goals, but who is intelligent enough to accept help and useful advice.

2 Extensions

Extension 1

Book: *Effective Decision-Making*
Author: J. Adair
Publisher: Pan (Business/Management), London, 1985

In addition to this Extension, you may be interested to watch a series of videos produced by The Open College entitled *In Charge*. These illustrate a number of aspects of supervisory work.

This Extension and the videos can be taken up via your Support Centre. They will arrange for you to have access to them. However, it may be more convenient to check out the materials with your personnel or training people at work – they could well give your access. There are good reasons for approaching your own people as, by doing so, they will become aware of your continuing interest in the subject and you will be able to involve them in your development.

ACTION PLAN

Work out your own plan of action for improving the quality and effectiveness of your decisions by responding to the following check questions and picking up the ■ action prompts.

Check questions

Your response and intended action

1 How often do you make decisions which you later need to alter or retract?

_____

_____

■ *A first useful step in improving your decision making is to admit to yourself how well – or how badly – you make decisions at present.*

2 How frequently do you make decisions without bothering to become well enough informed?

_____

_____

■ *Most decisions at work are based on inadequate information. You only make your life more difficult if you ignore information that is available to you.*

3 How much of your day is spent in careful systematic thought, as opposed to 'thinking while working'?

_____

_____

■ *Why not reorganize your day so that you can set aside some time to think through your problems in a methodical manner and plan ahead better?*

4 How well do you deal with interruptions?

_____

_____

■ *When you're a supervisor, life is often full of interruptions. It's pointless pretending they won't occur. But you can control them to some extent by refusing to be interrupted during your 'thinking time'.*

5 Are your intuitive decisions generally the right ones?

_____

_____

■ *As we've discussed, decisions based on intuition are often good ones, especially when there's a solid basis of experience behind them. But unless your instinct usually turns out to be correct, you may do better to rely on it less.*

6 Do you make a habit of watching out for problems?

_____

_____

■ *Anticipation of problems is always preferable to being caught unawares. It's a good habit to adopt.*

Action

7 How often do you write down your problems

_____

_____

◼ *That's another good habit, because writing things down often helps to clarify a problem.*

8 How often do you talk through your problems with friends, relations or colleagues?

_____

_____

◼ *Talking things over with a sympathetic listener can often have the effect of making decisions much easier.*

9 To what extent do you delegate your decisions?

_____

_____

◼ *Giving more responsibility to your team members can make your job easier and their working life richer.*

10 When you have a decision to make, do you generally have a clear idea of what you want to achieve?

_____

_____

◼ *Knowing what you want to achieve is half the battle. Get into the habit of setting down your objectives clearly.*

11 Would you call yourself a perfectionist or a realist?

_____

_____

◼ *Some people are always aiming at perfection; others 'muddle through'. Decisions involve compromises, more often than not, but that doesn't mean you have to compromise your principles.*

12 What methods do you use to get new ideas about a subject?

_____

_____

◼ *Check through the suggestions in section 2 Part C of the unit.*

13 Which sources of information do you make use of?

_____

_____

◼ *Look again at both the diagram in section 2 Part C and the work-based assignment.*